THE

richard wilbur

DISAPPEARING

illustrated by
david diaz

ALPHABET

harcourt brace & company

san diego • new york • london

Library of Congress Cataloging-in-Publication Data
Wilbur, Richard, 1921–
The disappearing alphabet/Richard Wilbur; illustrated by David Diaz.
p. cm.
Summary: A collection of twenty-six short poems pondering what the world would
be like if any letters of the alphabet should disappear.
ISBN 0-15-201470-5
1. English language—Alphabet—Juvenile poetry. 2. Children's poetry, American.
[1. Alphabet—Poetry. 2. American poetry.]
I. Diaz, David, ill. II. Title.
PS3545.I32165D5 1998
811'.52—dc21   97-24617

First edition
A C E F D B
Printed in Hong Kong

For Liam and Amelia
—R. W.

To Elizabeth
—D. D.

If the alphabet began to disappear,

Some words would soon look raggedy and queer

(Like QUIRREL, HIMPANZEE, and CHOOCHOO-TRAI),

While others would entirely fade away;

And since it is by words that we construe

The world, the world would start to vanish, too!

Good heavens! It would be an awful mess

If everything dissolved to nothingness!

Be careful, then, my friends, and do not let

Anything happen to the alphabet.

What if there were no letter **A**?
Cows would eat HY instead of HAY.
What's HY? It's an unheard-of diet,
And cows are happy not to try it.

In the word DUMB, the letter **B** is mute,

But elsewhere its importance is acute.

If it were absent, say, from BAT and BALL,

There'd be no big or little leagues AT ALL.

If there were no such thing as C,
Whole symphonies would be off key,
And under every nut-tree, you'd
See HIPMUNKS gathering winter food.

If **D** did not exist, some creatures might
Wish, like the Dodo bird, to fade from sight.
For instance, any self-respecting DUCK
Would rather be extinct than be an UCK.

The lordly ELEPHANT is one whom we
Would have no name for if there were no E,
And how it would offend him, were we to
Greet him as "Bud," or "Big Boy," or "Hey, you!"
The ELEPHANT is thick-skinned, but I'll bet
That that's a thing he never would forget.

Hail, letter F! If it were not for you,
Our raincoats would be merely "WATERPROO,"
And that is such a stupid word, I doubt
That it would help to keep the water out.

If **G** did not exist, the color GREEN

Would have to vanish from the rural scene.

Would oak trees, then, be blue, and pastures pink?

We would turn green at such a sight, I think.

An **H** can be too scared to speak, almost.

In *gloomy* words like GHASTLY, GHOUL, and GHOST,

The sound of H can simply not be heard.

But how it loves to say a *cheerful* word

Like HEALTH, or HAPPINESS, or HOLIDAY!

Or HALLELUJAH! Or HIP, HIP, HURRAY!

Without the letter , there'd be
No word for your IDENTITY,
And so you'd find it very tough
To tell yourself from other stuff.
Sometimes, perhaps, you'd think yourself
A jam-jar on the pantry shelf.
Sometimes you'd make a ticking sound
And slowly move your hands around.
Sometimes you'd lie down like a rug,
Expecting to be vacuumed. Ugh!
Surely, my friends, you now see why
We need to keep the letter I.

If, all at once, there were no letter J,
A cloud of big blue birds might fly away,
And though they'd been an angry, raucous crew,
I think that I would miss them, wouldn't you?

M is a letter, but it alternates

As a *Roman numeral* often found in dates.

If M should vanish, we would lose, my dears,

MINCE PIE, MARSHMALLOWS, and a thousand years.

No ? In such a state of things,
Birds would have WIGS instead of WINGS,
And though a wig might suit the *Owl,*
Who is a staid and judgelike fowl,
Most birds would rather fly than wear
A mat of artificial hair.
What would our proud *Bald Eagle* say
If he were offered a toupee?
I think it would be better, then,
For us to keep the letter N.

What if the letter Q should be destroyed?

Millions of U's would then be unemployed.

For Q and U belong like *tick* and *tock*,

Except, of course, in places like Iraq.

What if there were no **R**? Your boat, I fear
Would have no RUDDER, and so you couldn't steer.
How helplessly you'd drift, then, and be borne
Through churning seas, and swept around the Horn!
But happily you couldn't come to grief
On ROCKS, or run aground upon a REEF.

What if the letter **S** were missing?
COBRAS would have no way of hissing,
And all their kin would have to take
The name of ERPENT or of NAKE.

At breakfast time, the useful letter T
Preserves us all from eating SHREDDED WHEA.

What if there were no letter **W**?
The WEREWOLF would no longer trouble you,
And you'd be free of many evils
Like WARTS, and WEARINESS, and WEEVILS.
But then there'd be (*alas!*) no sweet
WATERMELONS for you to eat.*

*What's more, I guess there'd have to be a
Different shape in CASSIOPEIA.

The letter **X** will never disappear.

The more you cross it out, the more it's here.

But if it vanished, treasure maps would not

Have anything with which to *mark the spot,*

And treasure isles would ring with the despair

Of puzzled pirates digging everywhere.

Lacking the letter **y**, I guess

We'd have no way of saying YES,

Or even saying MAYBE, and so

There'd be no answer left but *No*.

How horrible! Who wants to live

A life so very negative,

Refusing presents, raspberry ice,

Fudge cake, and everything that's nice?

Because they're always BUZZING, honey bees
Could not be with us if there were no **Z**'s,
And many Z's are needed, furthermore,
When people feel the need to SNOOZE and snore.
Long live the Z, then! Not for any money
Would I give up such things as *sleep* and *honey*.

The illustrations in this book were created
on the computer utilizing Adobe Photoshop.
The display type was set in Birch.
The text type was set in Kennerley.
Color separations by Bright Arts, Ltd., Hong Kong
Printed by South China Printing Company, Ltd., Hong Kong
This book was printed on totally chlorine-free Nymolla Matte Art paper.
Production supervision by Stanley Redfern
Designed by Lisa Peters and David Diaz